PINK ORCHIDS

Patrick Cash

PINK ORCHIDS

OBERON BOOKS
LONDON

WWW.OBERONBOOKS.COM

First published in 2016 by Oberon Books Ltd
521 Caledonian Road, London N7 9RH
Tel: +44 (0) 20 7607 3637 / Fax: +44 (0) 20 7607 3629
e-mail: info@oberonbooks.com
www.oberonbooks.com

PB ISBN: 9781786820648
E ISBN: 9781786820655

Front cover photo by Dionysis Livanis
Back cover photo by ren at Morguefile.com

eBook conversion by CPI Group (UK) Ltd, Croydon, CR0 4YY.

'Sex, lies and cupcakes – the five cleverly intertwined monologues of Patrick Cash's play give a surprising twist to the idea that talking about HIV has to be all gloom and trauma. Sure, there is sadness, wreckage and rage – but there is also life, love and a lot of laughter.'

Neil Bartlett

Contents

Pink Orchids premiered as *The HIV Monologues* at Miranda London, the Ace Hotel, on 22 October 2016 with the following cast:

Denholm Spurr (Alex, pictured on cover)

Charly Flyte (Irene)

Sean Hart (Nick, pictured on cover)

Jonathan Blake (Barney)

Directed by Luke Davies, a Dragonflies Theatre production (www.dragonfliestheatre.co.uk)

Lighting design by Richard Desmond

1. Alex

He's just my type. Tall, dark and rocking a sexfestual pair of Levi 501s. Thank you Tinder, all is forgiven! I adopt this James Dean crotch-thrusting swagger over to the bar, but then worry that I look like I'm bow-legged and give up halfway through.

"Alex?" he says.

"That's my name. Don't wear it out."

Why did I say that? Why on earth did I say that?

"Nick," he smiles and shakes my hand – firm grip – and my heart melts into the floor. "Would you like a drink?"

Say something sexy and flirtatious.

"I'll have a Sex on the Beach," I say, batting my eyelashes. "*Extra* strong."

The new barman doesn't know what's in a Sex on the Beach; neither does Nick, and neither do I, though obviously I can't admit that, and so I randomly choose a bunch of spirits and hope for the best. As the barman is mixing, Nick and I stand at the bar in a neverending silence. I literally have nothing to say. I have never known a word in my life: what is a word? Maybe that's something I could say as an ice breaker: "so, what is a word?" No, that would sound weird.

Suddenly Nick says:

"Do you want a packet of crisps?"

"I don't really like crisps."

"Oh."

"It's because of the crunchy residue afterwards that you pick out of your teeth."

"Yeah."

We return to our terrible silence.

"So," I say. "What's it like working in tax?"

"Everyone's childhood dream. What's it like being an actor?"

"Rewarding. Very, very rewarding. Just not financially… I mean, not right now. But it's not like I'm on the breadline or anything."

I'm a month behind on my rent, and I'm living off baked beans.

"I've got an audition tomorrow though actually…
In a hospital."

"Do you get many auditions in hospitals?"

"No, sirree. But the writer's, like, dying, and the piece he sent over is about love and flowers, and it's *beautiful*, and as a serious actor I just can't keep away from, you know, tragedy, grief and devastation."

He hasn't been checking out my muscles and I'm worried that my vest isn't slutty enough – I *knew* I should have worn the Power Bottom singlet – when he says:

"I'd like to see you act."

And he blushes, and suddenly it's not as awkward.

"Fuck it," I say, and touch his hand. "Let's go wild and get a packet of crisps."

*

An utterly revolting cocktail later – note to self: Baileys mixed with orange juice makes the drink curdle – and I'm practically giving my straw a blowjob as I'm gazing dreamily into Nick's eyes. We have discovered mutual passions: *Harry Potter*, Britney and gay porn. Basically husband material.

"You know what I've always wondered," I'm saying. "Would Dumbledore be a top or a bottom?"

"Isn't he like six hundred years old?" asks Nick. "He's probably into kink by now."

I laugh.

"Wouldn't you have loved being at Hogwarts?"

Nick shifts uneasily.

"I worry I'd be selected for Slytherin."

"No, you'd totally be Gryffindor."

He grins wryly into his wine.

"Because I'm tall?"

"No, because you helped your sister through her cancer, which makes you noble, and you gave money to the homeless guy outside, which is kind."

He looks up and blinks softly.

"That's the sweetest thing I've heard in a while."

I wink.

"Babes, I've got sweet running through me like a stick of rock."

I avoid adding "just waiting for you to suck it out", but I believe he gets the message and we both drink deep, keeping eye contact over our glasses.

*

At the end of the third drink, Nick takes my fingers in his.

"I've never met somebody I feel such a connection with," he says.

Omg, he's fallen in love with me over a bottle of Pinot Grigio and two packets of Flame Grilled Steak McCoy's – that's quick even by gay standards. And then I wonder: am I in love with him? He does have very pretty eyelashes, but should that be a basis for spending the rest of your life together? Well, I can think of worse.

"I have to tell you something."

I'm just conjuring visions of us on our honeymoon wandering the spotless sands of Hawaii – or, you know, Bournemouth depending on how many acting jobs have come in by 2017 – when he says:

"I'm HIV positive."

Let go of my fingers.

I can't actually pull my fingers out of his grasp.

I try to remember if I learnt anything about HIV at school.

He's looking at me very intently for a response.

"Oh," I say.

"I was only diagnosed last week," he continues. "I thought I shouldn't come on this date but I was hoping I'd meet someone who understood."

Understood *what?*

He finally lets go of my fingers. I put my hands safely under the table.

"It's funny how you feel: like seven years ago I was this fresh-faced twenty-year-old just arrived in London, and how did that boy end up with an incurable disease?"

Incurable disease.

"But when you hit rock bottom, you can either lose yourself to getting wasted, or you can go forwards and try and use this diagnosis as a catalyst for a better life. And I wanted to tell you before we go back and do anything."

GO BACK AND DO ANYTHING.

"Thank you," I muster. "I just need to go to the bathroom."

*

I drunkenly stare at myself in the bathroom mirror. Does he expect me to have sex with him? Condoms are only 99% effective, I remember seeing it in an episode of *Friends*. I don't want to hurt his feelings, but I've got *shit all* idea about this thing. What if he tries to kiss me? All I feel is fear.

A eureka moment dawns.

I'll just climb out of the bathroom window and run away.

The window is small and requires gymnastic-like navigation. I balance on a bin and the hand-dryer before lowering my left leg through and swinging my shoulder under and –

I'm stuck.

Shit.

It's actually quite a painful position as the window catch is pressing intently into my ball sack. Each time I try to pull myself out I feel an intense twinge of discomfort.

There's nothing for it.

"Help!"

The door of the bathroom opens and in walks Nick.

"Oh, hi," I say, affecting a carefree chuckle.

"What are you doing?"

"I slipped on a paper towel –"

"You were trying to run away, weren't you?"

"No! No!" I laugh. "What on earth gives you that idea?"

"You're trying to climb out the window."

"I'm actually stuck in the window – could you perhaps give me a hand?"

"Fuck you!"

And he storms out, slamming the door behind him.

Well, I guess I deserved that.

*

The next morning I walk, quite gingerly, through the light-filled hospital atrium, and up to the second floor ward. I now have a bill for a broken window to add to my pile of red notices. A nurse directs me to Barney's room. He's very old, and looks very ill.

"Hi, I'm –"

"Eric."

He gazes at me intensely with his pale, watery eyes.

"No, I'm Alex."

Some recollection seems to shift.

"Alex. Yes, of course. From Spotlight."

He motions for me to sit down. Taking great care of my testicles, I do so. I notice the vase of flowers on the side and nod to them:

"Pink orchids."

He smiles.

"You liked the speech?"

"I adore it."

He offers me a plate of cakes:

"Mini cupcake?"

The bread had gone mouldy this morning, I was starving.

"Yes, please."

I popped one into my mouth.

"Delicious," I smile.

And I'm mid-swallow when he says:

"So you find me here from complications living with HIV."

Oh. My. God.

"I don't expect you come to many auditions in a hospital."

"Not many."

"But you do look like him."

"Who?"

"Eric."

He picks up a photo from his bedside table of a young man with blonde hair and blue eyes. I scan it critically: I guess there's a passing resemblance.

"That was before he fell ill, of course. And I've written a play about our lives."

"So you want me to play somebody with HIV?" I say.

"Yes. Are you positive?"

"Of course not!"

Maybe that was too strong.

"I mean I'm just not the kind of person who'd get HIV."

He looks at me.

"And who is the kind of person?"

I think of Nick and his lovely smile, and suddenly feel this huge deluge of guilt. I've been trying to text him all morning but "sorry" doesn't really cut it.

"I'm not sure."

You're losing it, Alex. You *need* this role.

"And the play will be funded by the Elton John AIDS Foundation, so there's quite a generous fee. You do understand though, that I want to cast somebody who has an appreciation of these issues."

The most horrific idea suddenly occurs to me.

"Actually, HIV is a subject very close to my heart."

Omg, am I actually doing this?

"My boyfriend Nick has just last week been diagnosed positive."

Barney looks more alert.

"Oh, really?"

"He was saying this diagnosis could either be a reason for him to stay at rock bottom and lose himself to getting wasted, or it could be a catalyst for going forwards and loving himself more."

I'm an evil, terrible person.

Barney leans forward:

"And have you been supporting him in this difficult time?"

I put my hand on my heart.

"In every way I can."

*

The next day I'm wrestling with shame, and consider calling the whole thing off. But then I open a letter from the bank charging me £35 for going over my overdraft limit. I stride into Barney's room only to find a middle-aged nurse making his empty bed. She looks up and involuntarily takes a step backward.

"Jaysus, Mary and facking Joseph," she says. "I thought I'd seen a ghost."

"Where's Barney?" I ask.

"He's moved on, love."

I feel this strange, unexpectedly emotional reaction. I stare at her, before sinking into a chair and starting to cry:

"But he had so much more to give!"

The nurse offers me a tissue.

"He's been moved down the corridor, darling."

I look up:

"He's not dead?"

She smiles.

"No, with any luck Barney'll be with us for years yet…" She's staring at me oddly. "It's uncanny though, how you look the picture of Eric."

I gaze up at her.

"Who was he?"

2. Irene

They were at his door again. I'd spotted the doctor on the right: fancied himself something rotten, he did. And now there they were, brazen as ye like, whispering and pointing through the window.

I counted to sixty like the sisters would counsel. But the anger was still there, and I tipped o'er like mussels out the pot:

"Get away from there!"

They stared at me like I was Mary Magdalene herself.

"We just wanted to see him."

"See him? Have ye no shame? He's not an animal in a zoo!"

The One Who Fancied Himself looked down at his feet. I had no real place to be telling him off, a young uppity nurse fresh off the boat.

"Sorry," they murmured, before slouching away with them.

I watched The One Who Fancied Himself glance back before he went round the corner. Never trust the good-looking ones, that's what my Ma said. Not that I listened.

Then I went into the boy's room.

*

He was just skin and bones, drowning in his hospital gown. If Ma had seen him, she'd have been marching into the hospital with a stew to put the meat back on his body. A mop of straw-coloured hair, and sleeping he had a face almost angelic. A fallen angel, anyhow. I was about to leave him in peace, when his eyes opened and fixed me with a stare, like cornflowers in the meadow.

I smiled.

"Can I get ye anything, darling?"

He gazed at me for a moment, before replying:

"I could murder a Mojito."

Now I wasn't expecting that.

"That might be beyond the NHS budget."

"Come on, I'll give you the money: a splash of rum, some limes and sugar. We're in business."

"You're supposed to be sick!"

"Exactly: drink is wasted on the healthy."

He didn't look more than a babe. We were the same age, I'd find out later: twenty-one.

"What's your name?" he asked.

"Irene."

"Irene, I am Eric," he said. "And all I want in the world is a Mojito."

I folded my arms: he reminded me of my little brother, Aidan. Wouldn't let it go when he wanted something.

"Absolutely not."

He raised one hand, with its purple bruise-like mark, theatrically to his forehead.

"Imagine if I popped my clogs tonight, Irene, and you never granted me my dying wish."

*

I was looking for somewhere to crush the ice. The shopkeeper'd winked at me when I picked up the rum. I'd said: "it's not for me!" and he'd said "it never is, love." The shame of it. I ran into a stock cupboard, found an old defibrillator and began whacking it against the ice on the floor. Suddenly the door opened and The One Who Fancied Himself walked in. He stared at me, the defibrillator and the leaking bag of ice.

"Bad moment?"

*

After I'd done my rounds of the ward, I went back to sit with him for five minutes. He was slurping the last of the drink through a straw.

"Never had a Mojito with basil before, Irene."

"Get away with ye, ye cheeky buggar!"

He smiled.

"I was supposed to start a new job this week."

"What d'ye work as?"

"Just a waiter."

"My Uncle was a waiter. Good, honest profession."

He grimaced.

"I want to be a dancer."

"What kind of dancer?"

"West End. My boyfriend's writing a show."

I blanched at the 'boyfriend' – just sounded so strange from a man's mouth – but I hid it well enough.

"Well," I said. "I'll have to get front row tickets."

"Oh, I'll save you two."

"That's awful nice of ye."

He handed me the empty glass of lime and basil leaves.

"Well, it's quite nice to make someone a Mojito."

I glanced around at his meagre collection of belongings: a photo of a man with mousey brown hair, big ears and a warm smile; a book on dance; some wilting flowers; and a plate of perfect little mini cupcakes.

"Those look nice," I said.

"My boyfriend made them for me."

"Wish I had a boyfriend like that."

"You will do. You're too nice not to."

I laughed.

"Lot of people back home wouldn't agree."

"Trouble, are you?"

"As much as ye are."

"Good. We're both trouble."

He was gazing at me intently with his big, blue eyes.

"Do you want one?"

I paused.

Then I took a cupcake and popped it into my mouth.

"Delicious," I smiled.

He gazed at me with an indescribable look before his eyes screwed up and tears began to roll down his cheeks. He turned his face away and opened his mouth in a silent cry of pain.

I touched his hand with the bruise-like mark.

"What's wrong?"

And he said:

"Everyone else said no."

*

In the canteen, I was looking for the news on Man U. Always reminded me of Da: most Irish players in an English team. And there was the headline: "Britain Threatened By Gay Plague." It made my blood boil. I didn't know how that writer could lay his head on the pillow at night. I felt like writing in: "come and see that boy in his room, and then you tell me with a clean conscience he brought it upon himself." He without sin throw the first stone.

*

The mousey-haired man with the big ears was arranging a new bouquet of bright, pink flowers in a vase. I was about to excuse myself, when Eric said:

"This is my favourite: Irene."

"Irene," said the man. "I'm Barney."

"You're the lucky man," I said.

"Oh yes."

"No," said Eric softly. "I'm the lucky one."

Then he turned sharply to me:

"Irene, Barney doesn't want my coffin cremated to *Another One Bites the Dust.*"

"Duckie, I just don't think it's appropriate –"

"Oh come on, can't you just picture it now: all those cretinous *Daily Mail*-reading relations on my father's side expecting *Jerusalem*, and then the bass kicks in. I'd love to still be here just to see their faces."

"Everything's a joke to ye, isn't it?" I said.

He looked up at me.

"Well, what do you do if you don't laugh?"

He turned to Barney.

"Irene was going to come and see the show."

"She can still come and see the show, duckie."

"She wants front row seats."

Barney reached out a hand to stroke Eric's hair.

"Of course."

"Irene, promise me you won't be disappointed."

"Now what would I be disappointed about?"

"That I won't be in it."

"I promise," I said.

*

His Ma rushed to his side, but his Da, his Da held back. Stood at the end of the bed, arms dangling by his side like he didn't know what God had given him limbs for. I came in the room when he was giving Eric a card.

"From my workmates," he explained, gruffly.

Eric opened it, then looked up:

"It's not leukaemia, Dad," he said. "It's AIDS."

*

I rang my Ma in Dublin that night.

She was full of the local gossip:

"… So she said 'I'm not going to take advice on the colour of my front door from somebody named after the tart from Fleetwood Mac', and I said 'that's no way to talk about Stevie Fitzgerald at No 37, even it was rumoured she once opened the door to the garda in her knickerbockers', and then Roisin at No 53 says 'did she not mean you, Rhiannon?' and I said 'dear Lord above –'"

"Are ye not going to ask how I am, Ma?"

She stopped.

"How are ye?"

I told her of the virus, and how we feared it could gain control of the brain. She listened silently before saying:

"Father O'Carey says AIDS is the wrath of God."

I paused.

"Do you ever see Angeline?"

"Who's Angeline?"

"You know who Angeline is."

"That baby did not have a name.

"She did! I named her!"

"She was a bastard born in sin!"

"She was my baby!"

And she hung up the line.

*

His CD4 counts had dropped to double figures. The lesions had spread from his hand to his arms, and on to his lower back. He'd developed shingles on the phrenic nerve, so that his thin, little body would be wracked by coughs, like a cloth wrung over water. The One Who Fancied Himself told me it was a matter of weeks. I could try to keep him comfortable.

I found Barney helping him into a pair of leather trousers.

"What in God's damnation d'ye think you're doing?"

Eric, clinging on to Barney, whispered:

"I'm going to Pride, Irene."

Outside it was a lovely, sunny Saturday. He was caught unexpectedly in a ray of midday sun, and suddenly his illness melted away, as he glowed for a moment radiant: a young, beautiful man setting out on the path of life.

I helped them climb down the stairs to the Fire Exit.

*

I never knew who tipped them off, but on the Monday morning there were people outside the hospital door. When I saw they were holding cameras, I felt knives twist in my stomach. As I drew closer white lights flashed around me.

"Is it true the hospital let a late stage AIDS patient out?"

"Why would they endanger the public?"

A million thoughts flashed through my brain: I was going to be struck off. I'd have to return to Dublin with my tail between my legs. I ignored them and fought my way through, until at the top'a the stairs, one of them shouted:

"Have you no shame?"

I turned to face them.

"Shame? Ye wouldn't know the meaning of the word. I'll tell you what shame is. Shame is writing about scared men like they're devils. Shame is spreading your lies and filth and *hate* without the hint of penance between ye. Look at ye! Shame is being blessed with your life, with your health, with your power, and standing outside a hospital door to attack a boy who's dying. Shame is carved like a scar in your faces."

I walked into the hospital doors, my heart hammering against my ribs like it might break my bone. Inside The One Who Fancied Himself touched me by the shoulders, then leant down and kissed me, softly, on my cheek.

*

My last image of Eric was on a late July afternoon. The setting sun filled his room with a golden rush, as dust motes floated in the light. He couldn't move for himself independently, and the virus would hook him into a foetal position. I looked through the window and saw Barney, very gently, brushing his teeth for him.

I drew the curtains and left them their privacy, together.

3. Nick

"And I just don't understand why he would climb out of the window!"

My consultant muses, as he brushes a non-existent strand of grey hair back into place. He's nice, but fancies himself a bit, too, I think. He looks like the silver fox off the front of the hair dye product boxes.

"Well, it is an extreme reaction. How did it make you feel?"

"Oh, I couldn't care less."

Dr Eros gazes at me through his trendy Rayban specs:

"That's a strong mentality."

"I'm titanium."

We look at each other for a moment, before I mumble:

"I went home and sent unsolicited nudes to every Hornet profile within a four mile radius."

"Did that make you feel better?"

"No. I'm giving up sex forever."

My phone buzzes on the desk with a Hornet message saying:

"Lube me up and ruin me like a Roman villa."

Both Dr Eros and I stare at the message, before the phone buzzes again:

"Destroy me with your weapon of mass de-COCK-tion"

Dr Eros says:

"Well, you've got to give him credit, he put some thought into that one."

The phone buzzes again:

"Expelliarmus me with your Elder wand."

I put the phone in my pocket.

"That's the guy who tried to climb out of the window."

"So he's changed his mind?"

"He messaged me yesterday saying 'if Britney can get through 2007, I can manage serodiscordant dating.'"

"And did you reply?"

"No, I hate him!"

"You have been talking about him for some time."

I pause.

"He confirmed my biggest fear. When I got the

diagnosis, my first thought was 'I'm never going to find a boyfriend now.' I just feel like I don't deserve love."

Dr Eros leans forwards.

"Nick, just because you're HIV positive does not make you any less worthy of love. We've caught the virus early with medication and your viral load is already undetectable. Physically, you'll be in excellent health. What I want you to concentrate on is your mentality, though."

He hands me a card.

"There's an event called the HIV Conversation tomorrow night. An outspoken HIV patient will be talking about their life. Perhaps you'd find it beneficial to listen."

I take the card, doubtfully.

"Thanks."

As I'm standing to leave, I say:

"If I do see this guy again, what do you think I should say?"

Dr Eros looks at me gravely.

"Well, you obviously tell him the words of one of the greatest philosophers of our time."

"What's that?"

"'You better work, bitch.'"

*

I struggle through the Friday afternoon spreadsheets at work. I'd told my line manager I had a dentist's appointment in the morning. How am I going to excuse all the future consultant appointments? I look over at Ian, back-slapping Colin with a lad laugh. Could I tell him about the HIV? His face when I told him I was gay. And I'm sure that's why I got passed over for promotion: because Colin goes for the monthly coke-and-wank nights at Spearmint Rhinos.

No. No, I can't tell Ian.

*

I swing by my dealer's in London Bridge after work.

"I was worried you'd given up, Nicky boy," he smiles up at me, lying on his unmade bed in just boxers, surrounded by baggies and a pair of scales.

I look down at my hands, and what swims beneath the skin.

"Oh, you know," I reply. "Special occasion."

He winks, and blows me a kiss.

*

It's oddly comforting stroking the baggie in my pocket. Now I've made the decision, my nostrils are itching for the sting, but first I head to Soho Gyms. I work my upper body until the lactic acid is eating into my biceps, and I can no longer physically lift the weights. My pecs ache with erect glory, as the sweat pours off me.

I take about a hundred topless selfies in the changing room mirror. I then spend twenty minutes agonising over them, until I choose one for my Facebook profile picture. As I'm walking to Ku Bar, I can feel my phone vibrating in my pocket with the likes and comments. I sip a glass of white wine, as I scroll through the likes. 30, already. The comments say: "marry me", "perfect", "dreamboat". I begin to feel wanted, until suddenly I think: would they still say that, if they knew?

Halfway through the second glass of wine, hurtling towards 60 likes, I wonder if George has seen it. I search for his profile and a holiday pic pops up of him with his new boyfriend. It looks like he's doing his sex face. I scowl and throw the phone down on the bar. I feel like messaging him: "you ruined my life!"

Then I pick up the phone, reopen Facebook, and leave the comment "it looks like you're doing your sex face" which makes me feel marginally better.

*

I'm tipsily walking up from Ku Bar to Circa, rubbing the baggie, when I start thinking of Alex. And then the anger rises again. It's just so unfair. Out of all the guys I fucked after I found out George was cheating on me, all those shags who fell into my arms and my bed; Alex, Alex felt like a connection.

Busy Friday night Soho swirls around me, and in all those people, I feel completely alone. I'm so lost in thought I don't notice Louis, until he slaps my ass and says:

"What's a nice girl like you doing with a butt like this?"

I look at his smiling face, and begin to cry.

*

Louis is French and has a *laissez-faire* attitude to emotions: wine.

He drags me to the Dean Street Townhouse, where he orders a bottle of Côtes du Rhône and we sit on the terrace as he listens. I'm not used to this, as all I've known Louis do in conversation before is speak as fast as a Kalashnikov. It dawns on me that there are two sides to every coin.

"And I've no idea how I'm going to tell my parents," I say. "It's like coming out as gay again, but worse."

He blows out a plume of smoke.

"A week, a month, a year: it's your choice."

I watch Dean Street bustle by in the late evening sun.

"You know, it's funny," I say, as I accept a cigarette. "I did everything expected of me: I went to university, I got a job that pays well, I found the 'perfect' boyfriend, I even got myself a mortgage… But I never truly valued myself. Not enough to want to protect myself, not enough to protect my lovers, not enough to wear a condom. Then on 30th July 2016, I was diagnosed HIV+ and I found I did have that lust for life, too late."

Louis says:

"Not too late. Trust me."

I look at him.

"Are you –"

"Six years. You have to name it."

"Name it?"

"You are going to be living with this forever. If you make it an enemy, you'll never be at peace. Name it, and own it."

"What did you call yours?"

Louis waves an expansive hand.

"Baby, what else? Paris Hilton."

*

I take the tube home and sit in the shadows of my living room, staring at the mephedrone. The profile picture has soared past two hundred likes now. I scroll through all those names, all those identikit topless profile pictures, all those clicks of validation, and feel blank.

Then I see Alex's name, and feel a strange glimmer of reaction.

I decide to take a shower. As I'm rubbing the soap into my hair, and cleansing my body, the demons descend to dance with the water's steam. I will never be able to wash away this dirt inside my body. I'm not good enough. How could anybody truly want me, when I don't even want myself?

I sink down to the floor of the bath, and sit with my head hung between my legs. Until I hear Dr Eros' voice, saying:

"You are not any less worthy of love."

I open my eyes. I see the crust of orange mould that has formed along the edge of the bath. The shower curtain is caked with dirt. Hairs and empty toiletries are scattered across the bathroom. The bin is overflowing with old toilet rolls, and the mirror is a mosaic of white spots from where I floss.

I stop the shower, put *Blackout* pumping through the flat, then return to the bathroom. It takes an hour, but I clear off the orange mould. I take down the shower curtain and put it to wash, I clear the floor and clean the mirror. Then I go into the kitchen: I do the two weeks' worth of washing-up that's piled across the counter. I scrub the blackened oven door until you can see it's transparent again. I take out the rubbish and the colony of fruit flies that have started living there. I hoover the carpet, and wipe away the dust, and the stains that have collected on the walls.

When the whole flat is clean, I strip off the bed stained with the fluids of months of men, and collapse into the freshness of new, spotless sheets.

*

For the first time since the diagnosis, I sleep unperturbed by dreams of swimming alone in the wild ocean. I luxuriate in the morning light for a moment, before I'm suddenly gripped with pure horror as I remember the 'sex face' comment and shoot up to delete it. I find that George has blocked me. And oddly, that feels like a release… I can no longer post bitchy Pop Justice articles about Christina Aguilera's career in the vague hope that I'm still communicating with him.

I spend the day messaging old friends who I've neglected, asking to catch up. Before I leave in the evening, I take the mephedrone baggie and empty its contents into the toilet.

The HIV Conversation is held in the Medicinema, with its array of rainbow-coloured seats. The guy who's being interviewed is apparently some famous writer called Barney, and the place is pretty packed. I'm looking for a seat, when I lock eyes with this blue gaze at the end of a row.

Alex.

He smiles tentatively.

I nod cautiously.

There's an empty seat next to him.

As I sit down, Barney begins to speak.

4. Barney

After Eric's death, I felt like I was missing a part of myself. But I couldn't cry. Have you ever seen *The NeverEnding Story*? 80s kids' film – always felt short-changed myself as it was only ninety minutes long. Yet in it, there was a creeping grey nothingness consuming the land. And that was me: a locked box.

Not that you'd have thought it, dearie. At his wake I was dancing to Queen, downing Mojitos and snorting all the builder's cocaine I could fit my great, greedy nostrils about. "It's what he would have wanted," I shouted to his bewildered relatives on the father's side, liked some dragged-up Marie Antoinette of grief.

*

James Hopkins Clinic couldn't organise an embalming in a funeral parlour, so I transferred my care to where all the self-respecting queens went: Chelsea and Westminster.

I nurtured rather a crush on my new consultant, even though he clearly fancied himself. Could have sworn he was a sister of Dorothy, if it hadn't been for the wedding ring on his finger – not that that meant much up Hampstead Heath way, let me tell you, duckie. But he was rather more serious:

"I'm afraid it's not great news, Barney," he said, holding my latest test results. "Your CD4 counts have fallen."

It was hardly unexpected: I'd lost huge amounts of weight, and the deadlines at work had become unmanageable.

"I'd advise medical retirement. We can help sort out your Disability Living Allowance. Although it's important to remain occupied."

I was still quiet.

"Are you okay?"

"Darling, I'm just trying to memorise this feeling. It'll be awfully good for the play."

He sat back.

"There's always the option of the Concorde trial –"

"No!" I said. "I'm not letting the drug companies take a gamble with my life. I've heard what happened in America."

"Those are rumours."

"I respect you very much Dr Eros, but I don't want AZT."

He sighed.

"Okay, let's see if you can tolerate Septrin, and if that takes care of the pneumonia, we'll then get you on Aciclovir for the rest."

*

I made a living will that I didn't want to be resuscitated. I ran a steaming hot bath, and placed the knife on the side. In a moment of camp that I, to this day, claim was simply *inspired*, I put on Edith Piaf's *Je Ne Regrette Rien* to bow out.

Edith was reaching her crescendo, I had the knife at my wrist, when suddenly I realised how much my mother's son I was – how could I let somebody else clear up my mess? I simply couldn't bear the thought of it, duckie.

*

So if one couldn't kill oneself, one had to live, didn't one? I joined the St Stephen's Volunteers, who held weekly tea parties in the waiting room. I baked up a mean set of mini cupcakes using Eric's mother's secret recipe. Blew that other queen's chocolate brownies out the water… Ooh, she was livid, duckie. *Livid*. I said: "don't go near the milk with that face, we don't want it curdling."

Years after I'd begun, there was this young, pregnant African woman. I remember she was wearing the traditional garb, oranges and golds like never you'd seen, and I thought it looked just *fabulous*. And I said:

"What's your name, darling?"

And would you believe what she replied?

"Generosity," she whispered.

I said:

"Ooh duckie, don't you be telling anyone down the bar at The Coalherne that. You won't get out alive with your purse."

I don't think she knew what The Coalherne was – lucky – but she had this lovely, shy smile. I offered her my hand:

"Generosity," I said. "I'm Barney. Now, tell me all about yourself".

*

I was agitatedly picking up the spliff ends.

"Spliff ends in a cemetery? I mean I'm all for spliffs, but honestly there's a time and a place, duckie, isn't there?"

Generosity bent over to help, but I shooed her away.

"Don't you be doing that in your condition. You'll pop. Go and have a rest against a gravestone."

But she wouldn't listen. And between us we cleared off his spot, where she placed the flowers she'd brought from her garden. We sat there in the late afternoon June sun as the trees were all a'rustling, and the birds were a'singing, and I said:

"It's quite a nice place for a spliff, actually."

She giggled, then looked at his grave.

"Do you miss him?"

"Yes." I looked at her. "But after ten years I still haven't cried. Does that make me an awful person?"

"No. Everyone processes grief in different ways."

"Are you scared of dying?"

"Not as much as I'm scared of my baby having HIV." She looked out at the shadows cast by the trees. "And I can't talk about it with anybody."

I took her hand.

"You can talk about it with me, duckie."

She put her head on her arms, and smiled.

"Thank you, Barney."

"Do you know what's worse? The boredom."

She said:

"You need a garden."

"A garden?"

"With a garden, you are always growing life, and you never get bored."

"What about if you live in a top floor flat, duckie?"

She smiled.

"Make your windowsill the prettiest garden in town."

We were quiet for a moment, before she said:

"Tell me about him."

"Oh, I wouldn't know where to start."

"What were your favourite stories?"

I thought, then smiled.

"Well, there was this one time, and you won't believe this, but the nurse comes up to him in hospital and says "can I get ye anything?" and Eric says, "I could murder a mojito…""

*

We'd been talking for some time, when my alarm beeped.

"Oh, it's time: let's see if these new tricks are worth their salt."

I withdrew a little pot of honey because, at the time, the pills were *monsters*. I mean, I can open my jaw quite wide – practise makes perfect – but you still needed a little bit of lubricant for the throat.

"Oh come on, duckie," I said to her, as she laid a thin drizzle upon hers. "It'd be awful painful down The Mineshaft with that approach."

And we knocked them back, and swallowed, when Generosity began to choke. She was clutching at her throat, and her eyes began to stream with water. Well, I had to do the Heimlich manoeuvre, darling, there in the cemetery – a 1, a 2, a 3 – and bang! It came out, but at the same time she clutched my arm and said:

"Barney, my waters are breaking!"

We were halfway up a cemetery hill. Didn't have a mobile in those days, duckie. I screamed at a dog walker: "call an ambulance!" and then I sat down with her by Eric's grave, and, do you know what, I felt curiously calm.
I removed her undergarments and mopped her sweating brow with my shirt and said "come on, duckie, don't panic" and occasionally said "push!" because I'd seen them do it on the telly. And when sirens were finally beginning to sound through the graves, I remember the sun had almost completely set, and I knelt between her legs and gently, ever so gently because I was so scared of harming anything, pulled out a screaming, blood-covered ball of life.

*

A week after the birth, I dropped into the little garden shop on the street corner. It played light jazz, and had stone busts of a rather draggy-looking Aphrodite. I instantly loved it, and wandered through the trailing foliage. In one corner, they had an array of the most gorgeous pink orchids: I remembered how much Eric had loved them, and I bent down to inhale one flower's scent.

As the sweetness of its smell touched my brain, suddenly I was there in the hospital with Eric again, putting orchids by his bed side. And then I was with him much earlier, suited at a wedding, as he made me breathe their smell and whispered in my ear they were his favourite flower. And then I was overwhelmed with his memory that I had stored so carefully inside myself: the night I met him in the rain outside that club; his fingers running lightly over my chest as he told me my heart beat fast, and I'd answered "it beats fast because you're here"; when he made a joke and looked to make sure I smiled; and his smile glimpsed only for me across a crowded room, when I'd suddenly realised I was in love with this fast-talking boy full of light and life and, without warning, there in that garden store the tears began to fall in hot, salty drops upon the orchids and I could no longer control myself as great, harrowing sobs of grief wracked from my body, out into the air, the light jazz, the flowers in bloom and the world that still turned without him with me.

5. Alex

Elton John is talking to me. Elton John is telling me he liked my acting. Omg, Mum is like going to *explode.* Can I get out my phone and record him? No, play it cool Alex. So I just sip on my champagne and nod along.

"… And when you made that speech about the orchids," he's saying, staring at me through oversized orange spectacles. "Well, I haven't wept that much since I wrote *Tiny Dancer.* And *Tiny Dancer* was a classic."

I cordially thank him, and take an unidentifiable canape from a passing tray.

"But there was humour back then too," Elton muses, as he stares past me into the heaving hall of Heaven. "Everyone always asks about Freddie."

I bite into my canape and it promptly disintegrates over my lip, leaving a great strand of treacherous spinach trailing down my chin.

"I saw him two days before he released that press release, you know –"

Elton is still musing to himself, and hasn't yet noticed the spinach. But now I have a half a canape in one hand, a glass of champagne in the other, and no conceivable way of wiping away the spinach. I try to subtly suck the spinach up, slithering quietly like Hannibal Lecter, without attracting Elton's attention.

"– and I said: 'Freddie, there's one question I have to ask: were there really dwarves with bowls of cocaine running around at the Queen afterparties?'"

Elton's eyes flick to mine, and I stop mid-slither in terror. Yet by some miracle he just looks away again and carries on speaking:

"And he goes: 'oh darling, don't be ridiculous. He wasn't a dwarf, he was a very small man. And have you ever tried to snort cocaine from a bowl? It's just not practical, darling. It was more like an elongated silver platter.'"

The champagne glass is abruptly removed from my hand and replaced with a serviette, as Nick materializes smiling from the crowd. I manage to wipe away the spinach just in time to join in Elton's roar of laughter.

Then Elton quietens and looks at me properly:

"And the last words I heard him say," he says, "were: 'but, you know darling, you've got to live a little.'"

*

Nick and I are taking refuge at the bar in the Departure Lounge, by an enormous vase of pink orchids. The whole club has been filled with them: evidently Elton's expenses account with the florists has been revived.

"Good party," he says.

"It's what you get when the Elton John AIDS Foundation sponsors your play."

"It's an important play."

"Did you find it difficult to watch?"

"Some of it. But you're very talented."

"Thank you." I look into his eyes. "I'm sorry –"

He smiles.

"You don't need to apologise anymore."

We watch the crowd tinkle, laugh, sip and swell in their finery. Amongst them there are any number of agents, producers, writers and directors and I know I should be networking. But I don't want to be with anybody but this man next to me.

Nick nods to an elegant, grey-haired man next to Irene.

"Do you think my consultant fancies himself?"

I watch the man look at her.

"Not as much as he fancies her."

Barney is leading a kind-looking African woman and her beautiful daughter through the crowd. I catch his eye and wink. He winks back.

Suddenly I turn, put my right hand gently on Nick's cheek and draw him down into a kiss.

*

I'm leading – some might say dragging – Nick by the hand to an upstairs part of Heaven, closed off from the party.

"Where are we going?"

Each time he asks I stop to kiss him champagne-drunk, heatedly against a somewhat sticky wall. It's like being horny teenagers. Until I lead him into the toilets at the very top level. I'm undoing the buttons on his shirt, when he says:

"Come on Alex, do you really want our grandkids to know that we had our first sexual experience in the toilets of Heaven?"

I stare at him:

"I can't imagine a situation ever arising where we'd inform them of that information."

I take his hands and place them on my ass, because I know it'll feel *great* through these suit trousers, and I can feel his resistance lessening in direct parallel to himself stiffening as I kiss him. But then he says:

"I haven't got any condoms with me."

In response, I withdraw a little blue pill from my breast pocket.

He looks at it.

"I've already taken my medication today –"

"It's not for you," I say. "It's for me."

And I put the Truvada on his tongue, kiss it from his mouth and swallow. I'm trying to get him to undo my belt buckle but he still pauses:

"How long have you been on PrEP?"

"Since I bought it online from India."

"Online from India?"

"It's pure. I've had it tested."

"It doesn't protect against other –"

"Have you got anything else?"

"No."

"Then stop killing the moment, and let's fuck!"

He's fully hard now, and as I release him from his trousers he finally gets into the mood, turning me around and dragging my own trousers down. I smile as he parts my legs, and rubs the shaft of his cock up between my buttocks, each time the shaft touches my asshole causing a corresponding swell in my own cock. He's kissing and nuzzling at my neck, his hands holding my hips, when he murmurs:

"Have you got any lube?"

Given I'd put some planning into this seduction, I obviously came prepared, and within moments I'm gasping at the cold liquid as his fingers gently rub into me, and then Nick is pushing into me and I relax onto him, until the initial gasp of penetration and suddenly Nick is inside me, and part of me, and around me, skin on skin, and I look round with my mouth to find his hot lips, as he pushes further in and he begins to fuck me, and the pleasure is building as he reaches for my cock with his fingers still lube-covered, and wraps his other arm around my chest to pull me closer against him, and the sensations flow in waves up my legs as I feel my orgasm rushing, and my sphincter contract and tighten around him, and he whispers in my ear "I'm going to cum" and I say "cum inside me" and we orgasm, there in the toilets at the top of Heaven, together.

And for the first time, I don't feel guilt.

*

Back in the main party, I intertwine Nick's fingers into mine, as we weave through the crowd. We don't say anything but occasionally we look at each other and grin with our wicked shared knowledge, and I realise I'm feeling quite, quite happy. I'm just getting us two more glasses of champagne, when we bump into Barney.

"Well done again Alex. I couldn't have asked for a better actor."

"Thank you for taking a chance on me."

Then he smiles at Nick.

"So, is this the boyfriend?"

My happiness turns to ice.

Nick looks at me affectionately:

"I don't know," he says. "Am I?"

Barney laughs, as my ice begins to crack.

"Well, you should know! I mean, it's because of you that he got the part, duckie."

The affection in Nick's stare begins to puzzle.

"Nick –" I say.

But Barney is champagned up, and overrides me:

"Oh, hasn't he told you? I've said it once and I'll say it again Alex duckie, you're just too selfless. So when he came to the first audition he told me about helping you with your diagnosis, and it just really won me over."

The ice falls in sheets and daggers around me, as all the affection leaves Nick's look.

"Helping me with my diagnosis?"

"Nick, I can explain –"

But there's an almighty crash as Nick drops his champagne glass on the floor, and is suddenly shoving his way through the crowd, running away from me.

*

I chase after him. I race after him out of Heaven, down through the Embankment tube, up the steps to the Hungerford Bridge with its white spires, and the sun lowering across the Thames. I'm trying to grab his arm "Nick, please –", but he just grabs his arm away, and keeps on going until we reach the middle of the bridge, and I can't run any further.

"Nick!" I shout. "I lied, I made a mistake. I'm sorry."

He stops, with his back to me. So do a large group of Japanese tourists, who seem interested in our altercation. Down the bridge a busker is playing "Every little thing is gonna be alright". But I'm just staring at Nick's back:

"I didn't think I'd see you again."

He turns.

"Does that make it better?"

"No. I'm still learning how to be the man I want to be."

Some of the Japanese tourists start taking pictures.

Nick walks two steps closer, pointing his finger:

"You don't know – you don't *know* what HIV's like."

I step closer to him, and he doesn't move away. I can see now his eyes are full of water. Another group of tourists – Brazilian, I think – have joined the Japanese.

"No, I don't know what having HIV's like, but I know what HIV's like. HIV is our sex. HIV has been our sex since the 1980s. HIV is the spectre and the boogie-man living in our bedrooms' shadows. HIV laces each kiss, and HIV lends fear to every caress. It's the guilt and anxiety of not using a condom. It divides and isolates us. It's loneliness. HIV is always there for us, whether we're negative scared of getting, or positive scared of giving. And it's so powerful that I ran away from HIV that night, when I think I was falling in love with the man who had it, because the next day I remembered every single word you said."

Nick stares at me. All the tourists are taking photos now.

"Isn't that a speech from the play?"

"Kind of. I adapted it."

He half-smiles, and I step forward closer and put a hand on his chest.

"But I want to be that man who can help you with your diagnosis. And I don't want to pass up opportunities in this world for happiness."

Nick pauses, as the busker sings "baby, don't worry about a thing", then kisses me.

attitude

What I've Learned Dating HIV-Positive Guys

This piece was first published on the Attitude website in January 2016

The first time I knowingly slept with someone with HIV I was 23. The boy was 20 and he told me drunk on the night bus home. He fitted an ignorant man's HIV stereotype: he was a ketamine-sniffing rentboy, living with a sugar daddy in West Hampstead. When I asked him how he paid the rent, he snorted and replied: "My ass."

He was also one of the nicest people I've ever met. I sometimes think about him and hope he's doing okay. After he told me his status that night, I said: "Sure, we'll just use condoms."

The next day I lay curled up on my bed, trying to slow down my thoughts. I knew something about HIV from the magazines and GMFA flyers, and that if somebody came inside you that was a big risk. But I wasn't absolutely clear about other methods of transmission. I remember phoning up the NHS Direct helpline, telling them I'd had my tongue up this boy's ass, and asking whether I needed PEP.

A lovely lady at the other end of the phone carefully but clearly explained: "No, babe."

Yet his status was why I didn't call up the boy again. I could deal with the drugs and the escorting – working on the Soho gay scene I was never very far from either – but the virus was one small step for man, one giant leap for my mind.

In the past six years I've learnt a lot more about HIV, and dated two positive guys. Let's call them 'Cute' and 'Sexy'.

Cute and I were drunk when he started talking about an abusive ex-relationship. "And he gave me HIV," he dropped into the tequila-laced conversation. I was shocked because we'd been friends before dating, and had been in many situations where HIV had been a prominent conversation topic. He'd never once mentioned his status, and I'd assumed he was negative.

Sexy told me at a friend's birthday party. Huddled together in the corner of a shrieking pub full of whiskey-soaked drag queens, he confided in me a status he'd told no one. Then I had to come out to him as negative. He'd read an article I'd written online and had assumed I was positive too. I kissed him and grabbed his hand, and stole him away from the drag queens to go home and have him to myself. His status changed nothing to me about him, but I was worried how he felt.

I wonder how many guys are out there keeping their diagnosis and medication secret because of stigma and fear. Like those guys who repress their sexuality for the 'straight' life of wife, kids and IKEA flat-packs, it can't be healthy to imprison such a storm. "Closely-imprisoned forces render and destroy", is the quote from Charles Dickens I learnt in sixth form. When I was closeted, I understood its truth.

Unfortunately, there are powerful reasons why a guy might keep his diagnosis private.

"An HIV diagnosis can affect the individual's relationship with his community in so many ways," says Professor Rusi Jaspal, Chair in Psychology & Sexual Health at De Montfort University. "Just one negative reaction towards one's positive serostatus can be immensely challenging to one's sense of self – it can compromise one's sense of self-worth and self-esteem, and as well as one's sense of belonging, acceptance and inclusion.

"Thankfully, we now live in the very promising era of effective HIV treatment that mean that a positive person's life expectancy is largely the same as that of a negative individual. Yet social stigma poses so many problems for the newly-diagnosed individual, who may fear rejection from others, the inability to ever have a 'normal' relationship, and who may continually question his own self-worth as he is made to feel inferior to HIV-negative people."

I've interviewed many guys living with HIV now. All of them have mentioned negative reactions to disclosure – either online or in real life. One 27-year-old told me: "A guy I used to know came up to me in a bar and said "I've heard something really horrible about you, that you've got HIV." I said "Yeah, I have" and he just turned his back on me and walked away."

Other reactions have included being blocked on Grindr, people stating they only date 'clean' guys, and being turned down for sex on grounds of health reasons. This is despite the fact that a HIV+ guy on medication, who is undetectable, is virtually no risk of infection – and a far safer option than sleeping with a guy who doesn't know his status.

"The key to dealing with this problem is a frank and open discussion about HIV: that is, more HIV education in schools, college and universities, and in other social contexts, so that people understand how HIV is contracted, how it can be prevented, and the implications that it has for one's life," states Professor Rusi Jaspal.

Patrick Cash

Acknowledgements

I wouldn't have been able to write *Pink Orchids* without the help, memories and trust of various wonderful people in my life. As ever with creating a work of fiction, the characters, structure and words are my own, but the emotional truth stems from many human flames.

When 56 Dean Street clinic manager Leigh Chislett told me his stories of being a nurse in the 1980s, there were many points I felt tears. The documentary *AIDS: Doctors & Nurses Tell Their Stories*, featuring Leigh and his colleagues, further inspired me by what lengths people would go to for their patients. I knew I wanted to pay tribute in 'Irene' to such warmth and empathy.

Similarly, running the 'HIV Conversations' at Chelsea and Westminster Hospital has been an illumination. I'd like to thank all the participants so far who have spoken candidly about their experiences living with HIV: Dan Glass (who named his Dot Cotton), Greg Owen, Catalina, Ben Collins, Robert James and Laura. You can listen to them all at: www.hiv-conversations.uk

And I have to thank Jonathan Blake, for allowing me to use choice, personal details from his own touching story in 'Barney'. And then agreeing to act it out on stage!

Conversations with friends both positive and negative helped shape both 'Alex' and 'Nick'. Denholm Spurr helped me make Alex into a nicer character. As always, director Luke Davies' intricate advice was invaluable. And Richard Watkins, a deeply treasured friend, guided me to a fuller understanding of the subject, self-worth and being gay.

Then there are the chats over white wine on the Ku Bar terrace with gay community expert David Stuart; the passion and fierceness of Matthew Hodson as he speaks; and Richard Desmond's stories and commitment to modern day sexual health. All the incredible staff at 56 Dean Street, Chelsea and Westminster Hospital and the St Stephen's Volunteers.

I hope I haven't left anybody out. But HIV is a constant learning process for all of us. And I'd hope in creating and weaving these stories together that what most powerfully comes out from the page is not the virus, not being positive nor negative, but our shared humanity.